Survival
OF THE Fittest

Survival OF THE Fittest

Keeping Yourself Healthy in Travel and Service Overseas

Dr. Christine Aroney-Sine

MARC

121 East Huntington Drive
Monrovia, California 91016-3400, U.S.A.

Survival of the Fittest
Keeping Yourself Healthy in Travel and Service Overseas
Christine Aroney-Sine

ISBN 0-912552-88-3

Published by MARC, a division of World Vision International, 121 East Huntington Drive, Monrovia, California 91016-3400, U.S.A.

Cover & interior illustrations by Ron Wheeler
Design & editing by Blue Water Ink

Contents

Why Worry?

W HAT YOU shared with us about how to prevent dehydration made a great difference in my trip to Mexico," related a woman who had attended one of my seminars on keeping healthy overseas. Then a huge grin spread across her face. "And not only did it help us, it also saved a Mexican child's life."

Another woman, who was about to embark on her first trip to Africa, asked, "Where can I find this information in a form as easy to understand as your presentation? The books I've looked at read as though they were written for doctors. They're far too technical."

I have been asked for copies of my notes so many times that I finally decided to put them in book form to help people maintain their physical, spiritual, and emotional health while ministering internationally.

My struggle to stay healthy while traveling has not always been an easy one, and my medical training did not always help with some of the very basic problems I encountered. This book is to help you avoid some of these problems. It is not a book on cross-cultural adaptation, culture shock, or training for overseas service. Nor is it about how to have a growing and vital faith. Many who are more qualified than I have addressed these issues. I have, however, given brief mention to them as they all have a profound effect on our ability to adapt to changing environments.

I was trained as a physician in Australia and worked in family practice in New Zealand for five years, but neither my education nor my experiences prepared me for life in the less developed nations of the world.

In 1981 I was offered the wonderful privilege of helping to design and administer an international health care program for the Mercy Ship M/V *Anastasis* and eventually for two smaller vessels, the M/V *Good Samaritan* and M/V *Pacific Ruby*.[1]

On the M/V *Anastasis* we developed three operating rooms for eye and facial surgeries and did medical and dental outreaches among the poor in Africa, the South Pacific, Latin America, and the Caribbean. I also worked for a short time in the refugee camps in Thailand, and probably have been exposed to the full gambit of health and adjustment problems facing both the traveler and worker in developing nations. It became my responsibility not only to recruit health-care workers from a broad range of industrial nations but also to orient them and the rest of the four hundred personnel on how to stay healthy while serving others.

Staying healthy was a challenge, as we were constantly exposed to unexpected and sometimes difficult situations. In spite of our best efforts, we often had to learn through bitter experience.

For example, during one of our early visits to a needy country, the local authorities told us that the water was safe to drink and that we need not worry about eating or drinking ashore. Unfortunately, we did not check this report adequately. Meals at local restaurants were cheap, so the crew flocked ashore in large numbers. Within a couple of weeks, almost half the staff succumbed to diarrhea and giardia. The dreaded "traveler's scourge" had hit, and it took weeks of stringent measures to eradicate the disease. We learned that what is safe for local people may not be safe for visitors.

On another occasion, I treated members of a team that had lived ashore for several weeks with no method of water purification, little knowledge of how to prepare food healthily, and, in many cases, inadequate immunizations. Among them were several children, including a six-month-old baby whose parents had never been discouraged from coming or given advice on how to care for the child overseas. When I first saw the baby, she was dehydrated and seriously ill. If the *Anastasis* had not arrived at that precise time with its team of medical workers on board, the story would not have had a happy ending.

This handbook has been developed with the memory of such incidents in mind and with the desire to help those traveling to the two-thirds world adequately prepare for the journey. Most travel-related problems are preventable or can be treated with relatively simple measures, yet most travelers have little or no instruction on how to maintain good health.

Working and traveling in developing nations is a stressful undertaking. We struggle with a workload that is overwhelming in magnitude, and we confront cultural and work-related shocks unequaled in our experience. The stresses we impose upon ourselves as we fill each hour of the day with work or play can sap us of the energy necessary to keep functioning in what seems to be a hostile environment. Fatigue lowers our resistance to infection, and we may soon succumb to the misery of disease.

Travelers to the two-thirds world need all the help they can get to maintain their equilibrium in such situations. No one wants their ministry to be diminished by a sunburn that results from inadequate lotion or by an attack of diarrhea as a consequence of careless eating habits. And the chances of catching a debilitating illness such as malaria or hepatitis can be greatly reduced by sufficient knowledge and forethought.

We cannot take all our Western health practices with us, yet we want to surround ourselves by as much as possible that is hygienic, safe, and familiar.

Another reason for writing this book is my concern about the cavalier attitude some Christians express when traveling to unfamiliar places. I often meet Christians who believe God sanctions all they do and protects them in every situation, no matter how little notice they take of the health guidelines they have been given. Sometimes they end up endangering their own lives and the lives of others.

My friend Mary is a good example. Several years ago she embarked on her first venture to India. Convinced that God supernaturally protects His followers in all encounters, Mary resisted taking any precaution from the potentially devastating health problems of this immense country. She reluctantly received the compulsory immunizations but believed a simple prayer would counteract any germs lurking in the environment. She ate and drank anything placed in front of her, sampled the delectable morsels from street vendors, and ate everything she had been advised not to.

She maintained her good health throughout the entire two weeks of her trip, which convinced her of the infallibility of her beliefs. Lesser mortals, who did not share her naïve faith and avoided all the questionable food items placed in front of them, still suffered the notorious traveler's diarrhea. They resented her confidence and glowing appearance.

But Mary's good health ended suddenly. Disaster hit as she waited in the Bombay airport for her return flight. She had dressed in a beautiful new white jumpsuit to impress her friends who would be waiting at home. Suddenly severe stomach cramps had her doubled up in agony, and before she could reach the nearest toilet a dark brown stain spread across her clothing. She cleaned her pants as best she could in the limited facilities and tied a towel around her waist to hide the worst of the stains. Mary had disgraced herself in public and learned in one painful and embarrassing lesson that none of us, no matter how strong our faith, is exempt from the attack of germs that surround us.

As we read the Bible, we see that God has always been interested in the health of His people, but He expects us to do what we can to protect ourselves. His earliest instructions to the children of Israel as He led them out of Egypt and into the Promised Land included guidelines for living healthy, active lives unencumbered by the illnesses that beset the surrounding nations. These simple, practical commands, encompassing such divergent subjects as personal hygiene, disposal of human waste, and care of the sick, are just as effective today as they were three thousand years ago. They form a good foundation to prepare us for travel to developing nations, where the knowledge of basic hygiene can sometimes mean the difference between life and death.

It is no good to cry "God will protect me" if we ignore measures to protect ourselves. God often protects us in our ignorance, but He does not save us from our arrogance.

This guide summarizes important medical information, which, when followed, can minimize your risk of sickness overseas and make your trip a healthy and enjoyable experience.

In health, as in all things, we should combine our faith in His ability to save and protect us with our own efforts to walk in the knowledge and understanding He has given us. We can truly claim God's protection only when we have done all within our power to follow the guidance He gives to prevent or alleviate our suffering.

Survival of the Healthiest

Visiting the Doctor

J ENNIFER SLUMPED listlessly in her chair and stared at the dirt floor of her little hut. Chickens clucked at her feet and flies buzzed about her ears. Her polyester blouse clung to her body in the hot, sticky air, and her left arm throbbed from the injection she had received at the airport. Although she had made a last-minute visit to her doctor for her yellow fever shot, she had forgotten to bring her records with her. When she arrived in Africa, no amount of persuasion would convince health officials that she had already been immunized.

Jennifer had looked forward with great excitement to this month-long mission trip, but it was all so different than she had expected. This was only her second week in Africa and already she longed for home. The tourist brochures had not prepared her for the dirt and disease, nor for the heat and humidity. She longed for a cold drink but knew from bitter experience that ice in Africa was made with contaminated water. She had spent her first few days making trips from her

bed to the toilet, a primitive latrine outside the house. She was just beginning to eat solid food again. "I didn't realize a person could lose so much fluid from heat and diarrhea," she groaned. "I wonder if I'll ever be able to contribute to the missionary effort."

Michael, on the other hand, had done his homework well. He was an authority on local customs, spoke a few words of the native language, knew to avoid ice, and brought cool cotton clothing with him. But Michael, when he got into a vehicle,

seemed to lose all of his common sense. He refused to wear a seat belt and seemed to enjoy the thrill of clinging precariously to the outside of crowded buses, even when safer alternatives were available. "After all," he mused, "if it's okay for the locals, it must be okay for me."

Jennifer and Michael are typical of many travelers who venture into risky situations with little awareness of the potential ill effects on their health and well-being. Paying attention to simple health and safety guidelines can make the difference between enjoyment and disaster.

Surviving the Pre-Trip Medical Checkup

In the early 1980s I worked briefly in the refugee camps in Thailand. The dirt and disease that surrounded me made my heart ache, and the pain and suffering of the refugees often made me ignore the health regulations I knew to be essential to my own good health. Water was scarce, so it was easy to rationalize my failure to wash my hands. Patients often relieved themselves on the dirt floor, and we had to ignore the smells and pollution.

Inevitably I succumbed to the dreaded shigella dysentery that affected many in our team. For three days I battled high fever, severe diarrhea, and vomiting. I would stagger from my bed, race to the bathroom, then have to deal with the dreaded "squatty potty"—a hole in the ground with no seat. The flushing system was an urn of water and a bucket beside the toilet. How I longed for the convenience of a modern bathroom and a flush toilet. To me, in my dehydrated, befuddled state, that would have been paradise. This remains in my mind as one of the most unpleasant experiences of my life.

Most of us are afraid of being sick, and the thought of being stranded in some unknown country far from medical help and the comforts of home is a fear that lurks at the back of most of our minds. Unfortunately, in an effort to deny these fears we often ignore them and turn our backs on the very things that will keep us healthy.

My initial preparation for that trip had not gone well. Like many people, I procrastinated and didn't visit my doctor until the last minute. I received my first typhoid shot only two weeks before the trip and, consequently, staggered onto the plane with the fever and aching arm associated with my second shot. I was dishevelled and unprepared for the experience ahead of me.

Due to lack of time I almost had to forgo some of my other shots. That certainly is not the best way to travel half-way around the world.

Before you travel, give yourself plenty of time to prepare. Visit your doctor two or three months before departure to have a medical checkup, arrange immunizations, prepare an adequate medical kit, and find out how to treat common illnesses such as fever and diarrhea. This may prevent many unnecessary and embarrassing incidents.

Early medical examinations are also advisable because some countries require proof of immunization before issuing visas, and travel arrangements may be disrupted if adequate time is not allowed.

Choose a doctor who is experienced in overseas illnesses. A growing number of cities are establishing travel clinics. They are able to provide better information and advice than your local doctor who rarely treats many of the diseases that are still common overseas.

If you are taking prescription medicines, including oral contraceptives, get enough to last the whole trip. In fact, it is wise to carry a double supply in case luggage is misplaced or stolen. Pack one set of pills in your hand luggage and another in your suitcase. A letter of explanation from your doctor listing medications in generic form is also recommended.

And don't forget the dentist. One of my friends went off to the Middle East ignoring twinges of a toothache. She awoke one morning with agonizing pain and a grossly swollen jaw.

An abscess had developed and a trip to the dentist became a dire emergency. She found one who spoke a smattering of English and explained her problem to him. He decided she needed a root canal.

Poor Joan. She hated trips to the dentist and found them bearable only because of anesthetics and the continual caring talk of her dentist. Here she received neither. The dentist attacked her tooth with gusto—without any pain-killers—unable in his broken English to explain fully what he was doing or why.

Joan's experience is not uncommon, but it could have been avoided with a dental checkup six weeks before she left home.

Dental care is often inadequate in remote areas, and pain from dental abscesses can be a severe and unnecessary complaint. There may be neither anesthetic available nor adequate precautions against the HIV virus. A trip to a foreign dentist is a little more risky and may be far more uncomfortable than any you've experienced at home.

Pre-trip Checklist

☐ Medical visit   ☐ Immunizations

☐ Malarial prophylaxis   ☐ First-aid kit

☐ Dental check   ☐ Check packing

Surviving the Needle—Getting Immunizations

One of the greatest accomplishments of modern medicine is immunization, which prevents many of the dreaded diseases that have plagued mankind throughout history. Although most of us hate needles, we must endure them to protect ourselves. Once the discomfort subsides, immunizations greatly improve our comfort and well-being.

Polio is a good example of a success story. Though the disease is still prevalent in some parts of the world, the last case in the Americas was reported in 1991.[1]

Ask your doctor which vaccinations you will need for the area you are traveling into. Here are some common ones.[2]

Tetanus

This disease causes severe muscle spasms and is often fatal. It is still prevalent in many countries but is effectively prevented by a tetanus toxoid injection every ten years.

Diphtheria

Most children receive this immunization as part of a routine schedule, but few continue the shots into adult life. If you will be spending time in developing nations, particularly in remote areas, a booster is recommended before you leave and every ten years if your stay is extended. If you didn't receive a primary course of vaccinations as a child, you should get a full series of three doses before leaving. This vaccination is usually given in conjunction with tetanus immunizations.

Poliomyelitis

Adult travelers planning prolonged stays in countries where polio is still a threat are advised to have a booster dose before leaving home, even if they received a full series of primary vaccinations as a child. If the primary series was not given or was incomplete, this should be completed.

Measles

This is a major health concern in developing nations. It is one of the leading killers of children suffering from malnutrition. A measles vaccine is recommended for all travelers who have not had previous clinical disease or immunization.

Typhoid

For the average traveler, the risk of contracting typhoid fever is relatively small, and the typhoid vaccine only reduces the risk of illness by seventy percent. However, travelers who will be spending more than one month in an area where food and water are impure should be vaccinated. After primary vaccination, a booster should be received every three years, depending on continued exposure. An oral vaccine was recently released which seems to provide greater immunity than intramuscular forms and is a great relief to those of us who hate needles.

Hepatitis

Several types of hepatitis are prevalent in developing nations. Hepatitis A, or "infectious hepatitis," is spread by a virus carried in contaminated water or food and has no specific treatment. However, a vaccination is just becoming available. You can obtain it in Canada or Europe and hopefully it will soon be available in the U.S. I think it is a must for any traveler to areas with poor sanitary conditions.

Hepatitis B may also be a problem, especially for medical and dental workers or those working long-term with children or intravenous drug users. A series of three injections will give adequate protection against this disease for at least five years.

Yellow Fever

Many African and South American countries require this vaccination before issuing visas, and others require proof of vaccination before admitting the returning traveler who has been in an infected area. This is often strictly enforced, particularly for people arriving in Asia from Africa or South

America. The vaccine is usually only available at certain designated clinics, and inquiries regarding its availability should be made well in advance of travel schedules.

Vaccinations should be repeated every ten years, and evidence of immunity should be carried with your passport, as it may be demanded at the point of entry into a country. If you have no record of immunization with you, you may have to be re-immunized before being allowed to enter the country. This puts you at risk of receiving an injection with an unsterile needle. There are cases of people acquiring Hepatitis B in this way.

One of my more frustrating experiences as a medical practitioner preparing people to travel overseas was with a singing team about to embark on its first trip to Africa. Everyone in the group seemed to be afraid of needles and made every possible excuse to avoid them. Finally we managed to get all of them into the clinic and congratulated ourselves for the accomplishment. Then two weeks later we learned that all of them had to be re-immunized in Kenya. Not one of them had remembered to carry his or her immunization booklet!

Cholera

This vaccination is not recommended today and has, in fact, been removed from the World Health Organization's list of required vaccinations.[3] It gives protection for only six months and is no longer recommended as a means of personal protection against cholera. Only ten cases of cholera have been reported in the United States in the past twenty years, and four of these patients had been vaccinated.

Tuberculosis

Tuberculosis is transmitted by bacteria spread through the air, usually by coughing or sneezing, by a patient with active pulmonary tuberculosis—an infection in the chest. It is the leading cause of death from a single infectious agent and already infects one-third of the world's population.[4] HIV positive persons are particularly prone to the disease.

Treatment for tuberculosis is inexpensive, although it takes six to eight months of consistent and uninterrupted medication. A BCG vaccination against TB is recommended in some countries, especially for children and those spending extended periods in areas where it is prevalent. However, the vaccine's effectiveness is controversial. An alternative, which is recommended even if you have already received a BCG, is a PPD test, such as Mantoux, which can be given before travel and then again on return. A positive result suggests exposure to TB and requires follow-up medical treatment. It may seem like a hassle, but if you are working in a high-risk area, it is well worth the trouble for your own peace of mind.

Other Immunizations

Other specific immunizations may be necessary for travel into certain areas. Pneumococcal and meningococcal vaccinations, rabies (particularly for those working with animals), as well as Japanese encephalitis for Asian travels, are some you should ask your physician about. The Center for Disease Control[5] in Atlanta, Georgia, will have information available regarding immunizations necessary for U.S. travelers. Ask your local doctor for advice if you are uncertain what is necessary in the countries you intend to visit. Immunization requirements may change as new vaccinations become available, so make sure you get the most up-to-date information.

Women who are Rh– and have Rh+ husbands and intend to have a baby while overseas should take the appropriate Rh immunization with them and keep it refrigerated (even if they are not yet pregnant).

Parents should ensure that adequate immunizations will be available on location for children who have not received primary vaccinations and will require immunizations during their stay in a remote area. If these are not easily procured, discuss alternative solutions with your doctor before leaving home.

Malaria Prevention

Malaria is still one of the most dreaded diseases of overseas travelers. Most of us have heard stories of travelers dying unexpectedly from it. It occurs in more than one hundred countries and is one of the most serious health problems we face in traveling to developing nations. Adequate protection is essential and combines the taking of preventative medicine and the avoidance of mosquito bites.

The most common drug used for prevention is chloroquine, which should be taken once a week and may need to be combined with other medications. The recommended supplementary drugs will vary from country to country and may change as new resistances develop. Consult your doctor regarding current recommendations. Also be sure to ask your local doctor, or a doctor in the country itself, about the presence of chloroquine-resistant malaria.

Be aware, though, that anti-malarial pills do not eliminate the need to avoid mosquito bites. Effective insect repellents (those containing less than 30 percent "D.E.E.T.") should be applied to all exposed skin and be reapplied at frequent intervals to provide maximum protection. These may not be readily available during your travels and are best obtained before you leave.

Clothing that covers most of the body should be worn at all times, particularly at dusk and dawn when mosquitoes are most prevalent. Stay in screened enclosures after dark if possible and use mosquito nets when available. Screens and nets should be soaked once a month in pymethrin to enhance effectiveness. If you will be spending long periods in malarial areas you may wish to purchase a net before leaving because in some places they are difficult to find.

Avoid using perfumes or colognes. In Singapore several years ago, one of my friends complained constantly of mosquito bites. One night as we prepared to go out to dinner, she sprayed herself liberally with some exotic perfume she had purchased. Unfortunately, it was as enticing to mosquitoes as it was to the opposite sex. It took very little persuasion

to get her to find another way to attract the co-worker she had been eyeing for the past few weeks.

These precautionary methods are especially crucial for pregnant women, who cannot take many of the prophylactic drugs and who are more vulnerable to malaria than others and may develop more serious side effects. Better advice, however, may be for them to reconsider their plans if they are heading into a high-risk area and are already pregnant or are considering becoming pregnant in the near future. Pregnant women who choose to go should make sure they are well protected throughout the pregnancy and consult their doctor as to other precautions they should take.

Now that I have suggested ways to prevent malarial infection, I should warn you about the natives' perceptions of our precautions. Sometimes the nonchalant attitude of locals makes visitors think precautions are unnecessary. Those who have lived in malaria zones all their lives are amazed at the paranoia of foreigners. They laugh at our efforts to protect ourselves from the mosquitoes; they just take a handful of chloroquine pills whenever they get a fever, often using them indiscriminately and in insufficient doses. But, to our consternation, they seem to succumb to malaria less often than we do. Unlike Westerners, they have developed some immunity to the disease and do not require as many preventative measures as we do. Remember, malaria is lethal and kills about a million people each year.

If you will be spending prolonged periods of time in an infested area, do what you can to help decrease breeding areas for mosquitoes.

For example, teach local villagers to drain stagnant pools

and to overturn containers, such as empty bottles, which provide wonderful breeding locations. A simple walk through the village cleaning up garbage and removing empty receptacles, like old tires, that accumulate water may decrease the incidence of mosquitoes and help prevent infection and death. Even something as small as a bottle cap can accumulate enough stagnant water for mosquitoes to breed. In some areas of Mexico, such village cleanups are the mainstay of malarial control and are surprisingly effective in keeping down the incidence of the disease. These activities make excellent school health projects.

Your care and concern for the environment will be a good witness of your Christian faith.

Preparing a Survival Kit

A medical kit is essential, especially if you are traveling to remote or underdeveloped areas. I suggest a kit containing typical first-aid supplies, such as band-aids, adhesive tape, hydrogen peroxide, sterile gauze, and cotton swabs. Also include insect repellent, sun screen, antihistamines, pain-killers, and, if possible, a portable water filtration unit.

Also take with you any medications you may need, including over-the-counter types. Medications available over-the-counter in foreign countries are potentially dangerous. Some medications that have been banned in Western nations due to their lethal side effects are easy to obtain in Asian or African countries. Others may have been on the shelf too long. Your doctor should be able to advise you as to what medications are helpful overseas.

Your local doctor may also provide you with several prescription medicines that can be used for a wide range of ailments. I personally recommend a course of an antibiotic such as trimethoprim-sulphamethoxazole (Bactrim or Co-trimoxazole), which is effective against many causes of diarrhea, urinary tract infections, ear infections, and skin infections. A good alternative is ampicillin, often one of the most freely available antibiotics in remote areas.

If you or your travel companions have some medical knowledge, you may want to carry several alternative antibiotics. Metronidazole, effective against giardiasis, the most common cause of prolonged diarrhea in travelers, and amoebic dysentery, is recommended especially if you will be spending an extended period away from adequate medical care.

Many people also recommend antibiotic creams. I have found however that in tropical areas these often have little positive effect on skin infections and the dampness of the cream may create an excellent environment for the spread of infection. A drying antiseptic agent, such as hydrogen peroxide, is usually more effective. Talcum powder, which helps dry irritating sweat, can also be useful.

Diarrhea is probably one of the greatest fears of travelers in remote areas. Oral rehydration solutions and Pepto-Bismol or loperamide are good additions to your medical kit to help deal with this prevalent problem. Remember however that *loperamide should not be used for children.*

Surprisingly, many people also suffer from constipation during their travels. This is exacerbated by constant changes in diet and fiber intake, mild dehydration from heat or constant travel, and sometimes just by the tendency to avoid using local facilities which are unsanitary. Having to balance on a dirty, smelly "squatty potty" is enough to make anyone ignore his or her body's demands. Metamucil or a similar laxative may be a welcome addition to your kit.

If you will be doing extensive travel by vehicle or boat and are susceptible to motion sickness, carry dimenhydrinate or meclizine tablets. You may also consider scopolamine patches as an alternative. These are applied behind the ear, and the drug is absorbed slowly into your system. The patches last for about three days, so they are particularly useful for pro-longed periods of travel. They may have unpleasant side effects, however, and can produce hallucinations, so make sure you read the enclosed product information carefully before using them.

Depending on your destination, there may be other medi-cations which should be added to your list. Antimalarial, antifungal, antiscabicides, and antiparasitic tablets all need to be considered. If planning to work in poor communities where you will be continually exposed to lice, scabies, and round worms, you may wish to carry appropriate medications. I also recommend antifungal cream and powder for treating athlete's foot or other fungal infections that thrive in moist skin areas.

For those who suffer from insomnia or jet lag, sleeping pills may be necessary. The effects of jet lag may be reduced by taking a sleeping pill before trying to sleep after reaching your destination. Ear plugs can help if there is a lot of background noise. In hot humid climates however they may precipitate ear infections and may be more of a hindrance than a help if you are already prone to these.

If you are traveling with children, you may want to purchase a range of children's medications. If space is limited, discuss with your doctor and pharmacist the possibility of creating appropriate child doses by crushing the medication and administering it in honey or another palatable substance. Be well aware of the different dose requirements of children as compared to adults.

By now you may think you will need an extra suitcase to carry your medical kit. In reality, these medications will fit into a shoe box or similar container. If you have packed more than this, decrease your quantities and use compact containers like Ziploc freezer bags. Make sure the outer container is waterproof. I have often had to wade ashore from a boat and have seen luggage end  up in the water. Even a heavy tropical downpour can saturate you and everything you are carrying. If you use Ziploc bags, store them in a well-sealed container safe from insects, rats, and other vermin which may find your medicines quite tasty. Also make sure they are well labeled in waterproof ink with the appropriate names (both trade name and generic), dosage information, and condition for use. Pills aren't much good if you don't know what they are or how to use them.

First-aid Kit Checklist

☐ Band-aids

☐ Hydrogen peroxide

☐ Sterile gauze

☐ Cotton swabs

☐ Water filter

☐ Antibiotics

☐ Antifungal cream or powder

☐ Metronidazole

☐ Laxatives

☐ Sleeping pills

☐ Talcum powder

☐ Insect repellent

☐ Sunscreen

☐ Antihistamines

☐ Pain-killers

☐ Water purifier tablets

☐ Antifungal tablets

☐ Antimalarials

☐ Antidiarrheals

☐ Anti-motion sickness medication

☐ Ear plugs

☐ Prescription medications

CHAPTER 2

Look Before You Leap

General Preparations

O NE OF the first questions that comes to mind when planning an overseas trip is "What clothes should I take?" Whether you are going for a week or a year, this is an important question to ask.

Before packing, make sure you know exactly where you are going, how close to the equator you will be, and at what elevation.

Prior to one trip to Nairobi, Kenya, I neglected to do my homework. I knew the city was almost on the equator, so I packed only light cotton dresses. I had forgotten however that it sits at an elevation of 6,000 feet, and the weather while I was there was bitterly cold. Never again did I forget to ask that

important two-part question about the equator and the elevation.

Many destinations in less developed nations do have a tropical climate. They are hot and humid and there is no air conditioning. In these countries, cool, conservative clothing is essential—lightweight cotton dresses for women and slacks for men.

Also be aware of cultural beliefs about clothing. In most countries mini-skirts are not acceptable, shorts are prohibited even for men, and bare shoulders may cause offense. And in many areas only prostitutes wear slacks, so be aware of the impression your attire creates.

Often the most suitable and economical cotton clothing can be purchased in the local market. On my numerous trips to Africa I have added several inexpensive, attractive batik dresses to my wardrobe. They served their purpose during my trip and were much admired on my return home. The adventure of shopping for such garments in the overcrowded, colorful bazaars typical of African countries is an experience in itself.

For church or business meetings, it is good to have an idea of how dressed up you are expected to be. A suit and tie is the accepted mode of dress for men in many African churches, even in the hottest weather, and the women dress in beautiful stylish African outfits. Africans have often asked me, "Why do Europeans dress so poorly?" I am too embarrassed to tell them the reason. It is because we tend to think that in the heat and dirt any old thing will do, so we take our oldest and dowdiest clothes. This does not create a good impression on local people.

There are other considerations as well. Loose-fitting clothes are more comfortable in hot, humid climates. Tight garments can cause chafing and heat rash or harbor moisture that provides an ideal environment for the propagation of fungi and bacteria. Long sleeves and long pants may be more comfortable in mosquito infested areas as they help prevent bites and reduce the incidence of malaria or dengue fever.

Other essential items are a wide-brimmed hat, sunglasses, and a water canteen. These should be carried at all times in hot weather. Hats and sunglasses protect you from the sun, and your canteen may contain the only purified water you see all day. During a recent trip to Israel, where the weather was extremely hot and dry, I read about a young woman tourist who went out into the desert alone without a hat or water. She got lost and died within a couple of hours from severe dehydration. If you are going to an area where water is contaminated, you may want to take your own water filter. You need a silver impregnated ceramic filter with a pore size of 0.2 micron. I often travel with a small unit sufficient for the needs of one or two people. Larger units are also available, usually at large camping stores such as Recreational Equipment, Inc. (REI)[1] or from mission supply agents such as MAP International.[2] Katadyn produces an excellent range from pocket- to expedition-size.[3]

A pair of good leather walking shoes is also necessary. Walking is an important form of transportation in many overseas countries and you want to be ready for it. You may even want to prepare by improving your fitness level and taking regular walks at home. Closed shoes are better than sandals and open shoes, even in the tropics. Roads are often dusty, and the dirt harbors such infections as hookworm and other parasites which can enter the body through the sole of the foot. Avoid walking around bare-footed.

Items for personal hygiene, particularly such things as women's tampons, should be taken along as they are rarely available in the two-thirds world.

Many people like to travel with a few items that create an "at home" feeling, particularly if they will be gone for an extended period. Familiar items can help you adjust more rapidly to the constant changes. Family photos, a poster of the homeland, or food items you can't do without can ease the transition into a new environment and often help ward off some of the depression and isolation that is common. You may also choose to use some of your precious space for professional or leisure books.

Last, consider taking an unobtrusive camera for photographing the landscape or the villages you visit. Remember, however, that in many cultures, especially in Africa, you can offend people by photographing them. Always ask permission first and be prepared to provide a small financial gift in

exchange. Also be aware that picture-taking may be prohibited in airports or in front of government buildings. Taking
pictures where it is prohibited is a serious offense often
punishable by imprisonment.

While packing, remember that you will probably have to
carry your luggage yourself. If you are going to a remote area,
a lightweight backpack may be more manageable than a
suitcase. It is no fun to trudge for miles along a hot and dirty
road with a heavy suitcase under your arm. If you are going
for a long stay, you may have no choice, but do be sensitive
as to the effect your mountains of luggage may have on local
people who have virtually no possessions.

You may have to ask yourself some hard questions and
make some difficult decisions. There may be things you not
only don't need, but would be better off not having. For
example, in Latin America many conservative churches do not
allow women to wear makeup or jewelry. If you will be

working with such a group, you may as well leave your jewelry at home. Find out as much as you can about these cultural morés before leaving.

No one packs perfectly the first time; in fact, even after many years of overseas travel I still leave things behind or end up with unnecessary items. Fortunately, there are always shops around somewhere to replenish my deficiencies, and though I may not get the items that would be my first choice, I am able to find enough to survive.

Packing Checklist

☐ Cotton clothing

☐ Long-sleeved shirt

☐ Toiletries

☐ Sweater

☐ Walking shoes

☐ Broad-brimmed hat

☐ Water canteen

☐ Water filter

☐ Bible

☐ 110/220 V converter

☐ "At-home" items

☐ AIDS kit (see page70)

☐ Bedding

☐ Long pants or skirt

☐ Dress clothes

☐ Cotton underwear

☐ Raincoat

☐ First-aid kit

☐ Sunglasses

☐ Mosquito net

☐ Camera

☐ Reference books

☐ Appropriate electrical adaptor

☐ Prescription medications

☐ Towels

☐ Special hand luggage items (see separate list)

Hand Luggage

I will never forget arriving at the Kingston Airport in Jamaica and having my passport confiscated while I frantically searched my suitcase for the address of the place I would be staying. Nor will I forget the frantic traveler at Accra airport in Ghana trying to convince the immigration agent he did not have a local address because he would be camping throughout his trip.

To avoid embarrassment and frustration, carry hand luggage to hold items that need to be easily accessed. Your passport with appropriate visa stamps, immunization record, and tickets obviously top the list, but a local address and phone number sometimes are just as important.

Other essential items include your medications, aspirin or similar pain-killer, tissues or wet wipes, a small flashlight, sewing kit and scissors, toothbrush and toothpaste, a razor and blades, comb and nail file, sanitary products, Swiss Army knife, and water canteen. Even for daily travel you may want to carry most of these items with you. Some may seem trivial, but having them when you need them can prevent much frustration and discomfort.

Hand Luggage Checklist

☐ Airplane & other tickets

☐ Yellow immunization card

☐ Passport

☐ Local address

☐ Facial tissues

☐ Wet wipes

☐ Flashlight

☐ Sewing kit

☐ Razor and razorblades   ☐ Comb

☐ Prescription medications ☐ Toothbrush & toothpaste

☐ Nail file   ☐ Swiss Army knife

☐ Water canteen   ☐ Eyeglasses

☐ Sunglasses   ☐ Hat

☐ Scissors   ☐ Pain-killers

Emotional Survival

We tend to think of health in purely physical terms and give little thought to spiritual and emotional well-being.

It amazes me how unprepared many overseas travelers are for their ventures into the two-thirds world. People are often ignorant not only of the culture into which they are traveling but also of the adjustments they will have to make. They expect overseas conditions to be just like home and do little to prepare themselves for the physical, emotional, and spiritual changes that lie ahead.

Each year about 150 short-term medical and dental volunteers fly to a less-developed nation to join the M/V *Anastasis* and participate in its work. We do our best to prepare these volunteers for the adjustments they will have to make, yet we always lose one or two who cannot cope with the poverty, dirt, and chaos. On one occasion, two young nurses decided to return home even before they had left the airport. The advances of the men, the haggling of the porters, and the rudeness of the customs officials were too much for them.

Life in Africa was just too different from home, and they were unable or unwilling to adjust.

All of us face such trips with a certain amount of fear and trepidation. We fear dirt and poverty; we dread the thought of becoming ill or dying far from home; we are concerned that our faith will not be strong enough to survive. Above all, we are afraid of failing, of not coping, and of having to return in disgrace because we could not adjust mentally, physically, or emotionally to our new environment.

These are legitimate concerns. Most of us know people who have gone overseas, enthusiastic to serve God, only to return within a couple of months, or even a couple of weeks, frustrated and disillusioned or sick and debilitated, feeling like absolute failures because they couldn't adapt.

I know of no way to fully prepare travelers for the smells, squalor, and misery of poverty or for the constant battery of new and often confusing and chaotic experiences that will impinge on their consciousness the moment they arrive. There

is no doubt however that knowledge and awareness of such experiences ease the many adjustments and increase the likelihood of survival.

Exposure to the heartache and degradation of poverty and injustice shakes the very foundations of our faith and it often calls into question our whole mental framework, including the precepts on which our lives are based. All of us need to adapt to conditions overseas—not by becoming immune to the pain and suffering but by adjusting our attitudes and expectations so that we can cope and work in their midst.

Here is my simple preparation list for emotional adjustment.

1. *Develop a theological basis for working with the poor.* Many Christians in industrialized nations are so caught up in the theology that God desires to bless and provide for them that they have little basis for understanding poverty and the Christian's responsibility to the poor. I have known many workers in poor communities who struggle with the questions "Why are people poor?" and, particularly, "Why are *Christians* poor?"

Those who answer these questions before they go will adjust much more rapidly.

2. *Place yourself in situations at home that prepare you for difficult and different environments. Build up the expectation that everything will be different.* We all struggle with unpalatable food and uncomfortable, unairconditioned quarters. We cringe at the sight of so much dirt and disease. We fight with roommates who want to stay up late when we need an early night.

It is not wrong to have such reactions; what is important is our ability to adjust and adapt when these situations occur.

During my years of service on the *Anastasis,* I spent several weeks at a time traveling away from the ship. During those intervals, the cockroaches would breed voraciously in the drains beneath my cabin. For the first couple of days after my return, showering was always a nightmare and my attitude toward it verged on paranoia. I would gingerly enter the bathroom in the morning and carefully examine every nook and cranny before entering the shower, looking for any sign of these nasty beasts. I would pull back and shake the shower curtain, where they loved to hide. Then I would flush the drains, hoping to lure out any creatures lurking in their depths. Only then would I hesitantly step into the shower.

On one occasion I no sooner began my shower than I felt a large cockroach crawling up my leg. I jumped out, brushed it off, and killed it with my shoe, then stood trembling for a couple of minutes before daring to reenter. I eventually stepped back in, and a few seconds later felt another creature crawling up my leg. I have never come so close to going home as at that moment.

One thing that definitely helped me cope with this and other such situations was the fact that I had spent much time as a teenager and young adult camping and hiking. My "roughing it" experiences before I traveled overseas were a definite asset.

3. *Take advantage of volunteer opportunities within the church and community.* Doing so will help you gain an understanding of how you will react when given unexpected and or unpleasant jobs to perform. A willingness to perform any task you are asked to do may be as important as your formal training. If your value and self-esteem rests in your job, you will be rapidly disillusioned and frustrated.

When I joined the *Anastasis* in 1981, the ship was in Greece undergoing renovations and repairs. There was no medical ministry and not even a functional hospital to work in. For the first eighteen months, I spent most of my time chipping and scraping paint in the hospital. We were so short on sand paper that I often sanded off the tips of my fingers trying to use the last corner of a sheet of paper. My hands were often covered in Band-aids.

During those early days I continually questioned my presence there. After all, I did not need medical skills to paint or chip rust. Yet a medical background was necessary to develop the ministry, and those hours of menial labor produced in me the essential spiritual foundations for everything that followed. I learned that God was not as interested in my skills as He was in my life and my obedience.

It is important for all of us, as we travel overseas, to view our impending experiences with this open attitude. We are not called to do a job but to follow Christ. We are not called because of our skills but because of our obedience. Flexibility is often the key to success, and a willingness to do anything we are asked may be one of the most important attributes we can cultivate before taking such a trip.

4. *Learn to work in multicultural situations at home before traveling overseas.* This is important not only in relation to the natives you will visit but also in relation to the team you will be working with.

In this day of rapid global travel and growing international cooperation, we often find ourselves working alongside people from many different cultures and backgrounds. Not only do they speak differently, they also have been trained differently, and we find ourselves in constant conflict over the best way to perform even simple tasks. Though we expect this when dealing with local people, we do not anticipate it with our teammates.

Surprisingly, an inability to get along with team members is the most common reason workers leave overseas service.

I have seen people fight over simple procedures, like how to take a temperature or how to give an injection. Even our ways of making beds, eating meals, or sweeping floors may be questioned. These are the little irritations that undermine team unity and create barriers between ourselves and fellow workers.

When I first traveled overseas, I was particularly adamant about the right way to make tea. I could not understand why other people refused to heat the teapot or boil the water in spite of my constant reminders. Years later I found out that my rigidity had almost ruptured my relationship with one of my best friends. My comments were a constant irritation that she, fortunately, was willing and mature enough to ignore.

5. *Deal with problems you have in relating to others.* Many people arrive overseas with very unrealistic expectations of fellow Christian workers. People who have had serious problems relating in work and social situations at home expect Christian service, and particularly Christian community, to be the answer to their problems.

These people generally expect instant forgiveness and loving responses to their own imperfections while being unforgiving of others. Expecting co-workers to be perfect, they become angry and disillusioned when people do not respond and support them as they think they should. Those who think living and working in a Christian community will be like heaven, soon begin to think it is more like hell.

The way people relate at home is the way they will relate overseas. Those who lose their tempers now will probably be worse in another culture. Those who are insecure or authoritarian in their relationships will not change just because they are working with other Christians.

Those who are aware of difficulties in their ability to relate to others will do themselves a great service if they work to rectify these faults before leaving home.

First, we need to be honest and admit our failings. Then we need to seek help in dealing with them. If we do this, our time spent overseas will be far more effective and our emotional adjustments much easier.

6. *Learn about the area you are traveling to and the people you will be working with or visiting.* Learn about the culture, customs, and economy of the country and acquire a basic idea of the spectrum of diseases you can expect and the measures you can take to overcome them.

Often the only things travelers read are the exotic, highly colored brochures produced by travel agents to induce visitors to stay and spend money in wonderful romantic new locations. These brochures may give you an idea of how to spend spare time, but they do little to help you adjust to the culture or working conditions.

I always try to read at least two books about an area before I visit it—one written by a local person and one by an outsider. This gives me a spectrum of views. Finding such books may be a challenge, but your local library should be able to help.

Speaking to people who have already been to the area or who come from the area will give perspective that reading can never provide. Such knowledge may begin years before we travel and will greatly enhance our emotional adjustments and maintain our mental equilibrium.

7. *Find out about the concepts of time in the communities you will work.* Time can be a major area of conflict and frustration. People from Western nations have been trained in

a very time-efficient system. They arrive for work at a certain hour, do a specific job, and leave at a specified quitting time.

In overseas missions this is seldom true. Hours are undefined; work duties bear little resemblance to expectations; and working conditions are far from ideal. On top of that, people from Africa and Latin America don't wear watches and have a very different concept of time and of the need for punctuality.

There is nothing more frustrating for someone who is used to working by the clock than to partner with someone who says "Let's start at eight o'clock" but really means "Let's get it done sometime today."

8. *Prepare yourself intellectually—become a "World Christian."* Understanding global trends and events will help you anticipate factors that affect the people you will work with and the different ways people think and reason—an important understanding for those who work and travel cross-culturally.

For example, I doubt that many people thought the Gulf War would have a marked impact on families in the two-thirds world. Yet it did. Many workers from Egypt and other North African countries lost their jobs when the conflict began. As a consequence, their families, who had no other source of income, were pushed into a state of chronic hunger and malnutrition. Their plight is unmentioned in the newspapers, but their need is no less desperate. This and similar situations are well recorded in such publications as *World Vision Magazine*[4] and *World Christian,*[5] which you may want to add to your repertoire of reading.

9. *Receive training in general knowledge areas.* Simple first aid and basic car mechanics are two areas of study that may one day save a life, or at least make your troubles much less

frustrating. Or, you may like to acquire skills in carpentry, agriculture, or cooking. All of them can be important in remote areas.

10. *Learn about culture shock.* Don't think you are exempt because you will be spending only a few days in an area. Sometimes it can hit even before you leave the airport. The problem may be compounded by constantly changing cultures, jet lag, and lack of sleep. (This will be discussed further in chapter 4.)

Spiritual Foundations for Survival

Workers in remote areas regard a sound spiritual foundation as the main factor in helping them cope with the physical and emotional challenges. A strong Christian commitment and a faith that is continually nurtured by Bible study and prayer will probably help you more than all the travel or educational books you can read. Developing a good discipline of daily quiet time may be one of the most important preparations you can make. It will bear fruit not only spiritually but also emotionally and physically.

Speak to people who have already traveled overseas about their ways of maintaining their spiritual life in a difficult and stressful environment. Their insights may help you develop a spiritual routine that will stand you in good stead throughout your travels.

One of my biggest milestones in maintaining my spiritual life was taking half an hour, from 10:30–11 A.M., to pray and read the Bible. Initially I felt guilty for using "work time," but I soon realized that my emotional stability under stress, and thus my ability to fulfill my job, was greatly improved. Taking a short break to pray helped more than any other activity when I was feeling stress.

Studies conducted by the Christian Medical and Dental Society[6] have shown that our spiritual state and the strength of our Christian commitment have a positive effect on both physical and mental health. High blood pressure and depression are but two of the conditions shown to improve with regular spiritual observance.

For me, the words of Psalm 51:10–13 are a good "spiritual prescription" for daily use. These verses represent all the principles of a good spiritual foundation and always remind me of areas I need to work on. I often meditate on them during my travels, searching my life to determine if I am adhering to their principles. They are a good spiritual checklist to examine and re-examine.

First, verse 10 speaks of our need for "a clean heart." This is one of the greatest needs in relationships with people. We need to constantly maintain right attitudes and right relationships, admitting our faults when needed, and seeking forgiveness and reconciliation at every opportunity. Only when we are reconciled to our brothers and sisters and to God in all our attitudes and behavior can our hearts truly be clean.

The next principle is that of "a steadfast spirit." This speaks of the need for perseverance and endurance. Sticking power, the willingness and the ability to endure any hardship, is a constant need for overseas travelers and workers. Nothing overseas ever seems to work out the way we expect it to, or want it to, and it would be easy to get on the next plane and return home. We live in a day of instant gratification, one in which endurance and perseverance are often neglected; yet without these foundations we will never survive.

The third principle (Psalm 51:11) is "God's presence." Our mental and spiritual equilibrium is maintained only through constant fellowship, prayer, and Bible study. Without it we soon become dry and ineffective.

Verse 11 also speaks of our need for the Holy Spirit, the representation of God's power and comfort. The events and images we experience overseas often cause pain and bewilderment, so the comfort of the Holy Spirit is necessary for encouragement, sustenance, and strength.

"Restore to me the joy of your salvation," says verse 12. This speaks of God's love and inner strength. Our own reserves are inadequate to sustain us, so we need the constant indwelling of God's presence to renew and revitalize our physical and spiritual strength.

"And grant me a willing spirit, to sustain me," continues this verse. Willingness, obedience, and flexibility are all represented here. Without such foundations in our lives, we soon become disillusioned and frustrated.

These principles should be packed in our spiritual luggage whenever we travel.

Spiritual Checklist (Psalm 51:10–12)

"A clean heart"	Forgiveness and reconciliation
"A steadfast spirit"	Endurance and perseverance
"Your presence"	Fellowship with God

"Your Holy Spirit"	Power and comfort
"The joy of your salvation"	Joy and love
"A willing spirit"	Flexibility and obedience

CHAPTER 3

Survival Abroad

Enjoying the Trip

T RAVEL CAN be an exhausting and sometimes disorienting experience. Waiting for long periods of time in crowded rooms, traveling for many hours in uncomfortable planes, going without sleep, and becoming dehydrated by dry, recycled air can produce nausea, dizziness, and emotional swings. This exacerbates the problems of crossing several time zones and getting our time clocks out of sync. Adjustment to a new location may take up to two weeks, depending on how many time zones you have crossed.

Be aware of the effect your travel schedule will have on your body, emotions, and spirit and allow yourself time and energy to adjust. Plan your trip so you do not have a rigorous schedule for a few days after extensive travel. Your ability to think and handle difficult decisions will be impaired far more than you realize. If you suffer badly from insomnia, sleeping

pills may reduce your adaptation period, though they may slow you down during the day and add to your feeling of disorientation if taken too frequently.

North-south travel is often as disorienting as east-west travel. Going from long, hot summer days to short, cold winter days in a few hours can have as much of an effect on your psyche as changing time zones and is often responsible for dramatic emotional swings.

Survival on the Roads

Road accidents are the main cause of death in people traveling overseas. In Thailand, eleven missionaries—mostly women and children—were killed in an accident on their way home from a local festival when their van was hit by a large truck careening along the highway.

People who take every possible precaution at home often throw off restraints when overseas. They excitedly participate in the game of "how many missionaries can I fit into a VW bug," cling precariously to the sides of vehicles, and travel at nightmarish speeds they would never even consider at home.

Perhaps surprising to some is the fact that travel in foreign Western countries can be as hazardous as in developing nations. For people used to traveling on the right, simply stepping off a curb can be dangerous in a country where traffic drives on the left. Americans learn to look to the left just before stepping to the street, but in countries like England, the traffic is coming from the right. And in Africa or South America the situation may be even worse because you can never be sure *which* side of the road the traffic is on. Add to that the fact that pedestrians and animals have as much right to use the road as vehicles, and you get a fair image of how chaotic things can be.

You have probably seen pictures of public transportation in developing nations that show people clinging to the outside of vehicles. Such scenes are not uncommon, but the slogan on one particular truck caught my attention. Emblazoned over the driver's cab of a truck that had people perched on the back and hanging over the sides read, "Safe in the arms of Jesus." It summed up the whole attitude to road safety and the rather fatalistic attitude to life.

Unfortunately, foreigners tend to act in the same fashion when traveling in such countries. A good rule of thumb is to follow, whenever possible, the same precautions overseas as you do at home. For example, make sure that vehicles carry no more passengers than at home.

Also, sitting in the back of pickup vans is particularly dangerous and should be avoided. It is crazy to take unnecessary risks just because the laws are lax.

Remember, seat belts and helmets were invented for our protection, and they are even more important in countries where driving is chaotic and rules of the road are next to nonexistent. Wear them whenever they are available.

In Jamaica, when approaching any type of road hazard, you'll see a sign that says, "You have been warned."

How true. We have been warned; we just need to follow the advice.

Survival in the Water—Swimming

Most people enjoy taking a refreshing dip in the water on a hot day. In the tropics however this often is unadvisable, especially in fresh water where a variety of debilitating infections may lurk. These diseases are often easier to prevent than to cure, so keep that in mind when you are about ready to succumb to the lure of a cool stream.

In Kenya in 1984, fifteen of eighteen American students on a study tour contracted a disease called schistosomiasis after swimming in a stream. The infection, which is carried by a very small worm that penetrates the skin of a swimmer or wader, may cause intense itching and can spread to the liver and nervous system. If exposed, promptly and vigorously dry yourself with a towel and douse the skin with rubbing alcohol to help prevent infection.

Ocean water is usually safe, though it may hold other risks, such as sharks, jellyfish, and poisonous shellfish.

Since the beaches in developing nations are seldom patrolled, the risk of unsuspected currents and unpredictable tidal waves must be taken into account. Do not go swimming alone or take other unnecessary risks.

The *Anastasis* visited one Mexican port that had a beautiful beach nearby. Unfortunately, it had extremely dangerous undertows and currents, and there were no lifeguards on duty. We learned that at least one person a week drowned while swimming there. Since it was the only nearby place to swim, we encouraged people to go in groups that included at least one person well-versed in life-saving. Our solution encouraged cooperation and seemed satisfactory to all concerned.

Other problems occur when swimming near coral reefs. Coral and its co-habitors may be poisonous and can induce nasty rashes or severe illnesses. Sea urchins burrow under the sand and can cause irritating infections if the spines penetrate skin. Wear strong-soled shoes when swimming in reefs.

Surviving in the Sun

Tropical sun is very dangerous in countries on or near the equator, and with the thinning of the ozone layer, ultraviolet rays pose a problem even in "mild" climates. I get frustrated by people who brag that they never get sunburned. Most of them have never been exposed to intense ultraviolet radiation. "Toasting on the coast" can curtail your missionary service as effectively as any fatal illness.

One twenty-year-old woman suffered a life-threatening cardiac arrest simply because she was severely sunburned and dehydrated. Her foolish behavior of lying in the sun all day produced a burn every bit as serious as one created by a fire.

For some, fifteen minutes in the sun will create a pink glow; an hour will produce an uncomfortable burn; and all-day exposure will leave the traveler prostrate, blistered, and seriously dehydrated.

To block the sun's rays, wear a broad-brimmed hat. This provides effective protection for those who cannot avoid the sun. There are also many effective sunscreens on the market. For tropical sun, use at least a Factor 15 suncreen for adequate protection and a Factor 25 if you have a fair complexion. If you are determined to get a tan, gradually increase periods of exposure.

These precautions will protect you not only short term but long term as well. Skin cancer is a very real problem for people who spend long hours in the sun, especially those who have fair skin. Unfortunately, such skin damage may not become apparent for many years. Malignant moles are a particularly virulent form of skin cancer which still claim the lives of many unsuspecting sun worshipers.

The slogan of the Victoria Cancer Society in Australia provides excellent advice: SLIP, SLOP, SLAP.

SLIP on a shirt; SLOP on sunscreen; SLAP on a hat.

Travelers unaccustomed to tropical heat and sun must also take special precautions to avoid dehydration. Increase water intake when traveling in tropical or desert climates. Normal intake for temperatures of 70°F (20°C) is about three liters a day. An additional liter is required for each rise of 10°C. Another half liter should be added for each hour of physical activity or of sunbathing in the direct sun. Dark yellow urine is a sign that you should increase your intake of water.

One extremely painful outcome of mild dehydration is kidney stones. They cause agonizing pain, which is something no one wants to suffer from in remote areas. Keeping ourselves adequately hydrated is a good way to avoid such a fate.

Heat stroke is another result of inadequate fluid intake, especially for elderly travelers. Its symptoms are high body temperature, severe headaches, and confusion. The patient should be kept cool by fanning and sponging with cold water, and fluid should be replaced as soon as possible.

The sun's glare can also create problems, such as cataracts, so sunglasses are more than a fashion statement. They not only protect eyes from the intense glare of the tropical sun but also from wind-borne dirt, particularly in desert areas, which can cause eye infections. Dark green or gray lenses are best for filtering ultraviolet rays and yet preserving reasonable color discrimination. Look for those marked 100 percent UVB protection. Graded lenses, which often have little tinting in the lower segment, may be fashionable but they have little practical value.

Surviving Diarrhea—The Traveler's Scourge

Diarrhea is one of the main causes of illness and death in poor communities, claiming the lives of one out of every ten children in the world. It is also a major cause of illness in people traveling to developing nations.

If you travel long enough in developing nations, you too will eventually succumb to one of the dreaded "lurgies." Like a rite of initiation into an elite club, this usually marks promotion from casual visitor to accepted colleague. A person's first encounter often results from his or her own indiscretion: failing to resist the temptation to taste local delicacies displayed by street vendors who waft irresistible aromas in our direction; or succombing to the allure of iced drinks, such as liquados—concoctions of milk, pulped fruit, and crushed ice fondly referred to as "amoeba shakes" because of their propensity for causing diarrhea.

Major diarrheal-causing organisms are transmitted from the feces of one person to the mouth of someone else. Transmission can occur directly when infected persons handle food or utensils without washing their hands, or indirectly through contaminated water or an intermediary host of rodents, flies, and cockroaches. Infection may also be present on unwashed food, in dirt, or on any uncleaned object.

Unfortunately, most diarrheal infections are spread by contaminated dishes and utensils, and there is little we can do to prevent this. In spite of precautions, many still succumb to infectious diarrhea, the scourge of any traveler in foreign lands. It is not confined to the missionary in isolated and backward communities. It results from a variety of diseases, the chief of which is giardia lamblia, which often presents itself just as the short-term worker is returning home. Amoebic dysentery, typhoid, and cholera must also be considered.

The simple act of cleaning hands is perhaps the most effective preventive measure. In the book of Leviticus, God instructed the priests to wash their hands. We tend to think this was merely a symbolic religious ritual, but it may have had a more practical purpose.

Wash your hands as frequently as possible without becoming obsessive. Wash them after handling money, after touching possibly contaminated surfaces, or after holding children who may have fecal contamination on their clothing.

You should also wash your hands before preparing food, before eating, and after going to the toilet. Sometimes it is difficult to obtain a sufficient supply of fresh water for cleaning hands. Adding enough laundry bleach to water to produce a one-tenth percent bleach solution is sufficient to kill most organisms, including HIV and hepatitis viruses. Bleach is easy to obtain in most countries.

The second most

effective measure is to maintain a pure water supply. The simplest purification method is to boil water for twenty minutes.

If fuel supplies are limited, the addition of laundry bleach is an effective purification method. Add two drops of four-percent laundry bleach to every quart of drinking water, four drops if the water is cloudy, and let it stand for thirty minutes. Or add two water purification tablets per quart of water and let it stand for thirty minutes.

Another alternative is to carry a portable ceramic filter. These are particularly useful for teams traveling in remote areas and are available in several sizes to suit individual as well as group needs.

Remember, containers spread disease as effectively as the water inside, so clean them thoroughly with purified water before using them.

Bottled drinks are somewhat safer since the bottles are not as easily contaminated as drinking glasses. But even bottled drinking water is sometimes suspect. Some vendors fill water containers from streams or faucets, pretending to provide purified drinking water. If you buy bottled drinks, make sure the seals are intact.

Also, use only purified water to brush your teeth and to make ice. Freezing does not kill most organisms.

In regard to food, the Peace Corps adage is good advice to follow in developing nations: "Cook it, peel it, or forget it." Before preparing fruits and raw vegetables it is also advisable to bleach them to remove any impurities. A one-tenth percent concentration of bleach is adequate. If you are using four percent laundry bleach, this is a 1:10 solution. Bleach concentrations vary from country to country however so remember to change the ratio accordingly.

Avoid eating fruits and vegetables in restaurants.

Eating from roadside stalls is, as mentioned, an area in which all of us have our discipline sorely tested. The delicious aroma of local delicacies will tempt even the most seasoned traveler. Just remember that the miserable effects of a few moments of enjoyment may last far longer than the pleasant taste of the food.

Fish, oysters, and other seafood delights are also suspect as the health controls operating at home do not apply overseas. Raw fish and seafood also harbor parasites such as tapeworm and liver fluke.

Regardless of what causes a particular case of diarrhea, the condition rapidly leads to dehydration in tropical climates. Begin oral rehydration at the least sign of illness, long before a definitive diagnosis is made. Most cases of diarrhea are limited to individuals and require only fluid and salt replacements to bring relief.

A basic knowledge of how to replace fluids and salts may do more than simply save yourself discomfort; it can be a useful piece of information for others. Thousands of children die each day from the effects of dehydration because their mothers do not know this simple remedy. Your knowledge may save some of them too.

The easiest rehydration prescription takes advantage of local, readily available ingredients. To one liter of water add two level tablespoons of sugar or honey, $1/4$ teaspoon salt, and $1/4$ teaspoon baking soda. If available, also add $1/2$ cup of orange juice, green coconut milk, or a bit of mashed ripe banana.

Recent research indicates that starch-based solutions may be more effective than sugar-based solutions for rehydration. Not only do they rehydrate the patient, they also reduce the frequency of diarrhea. In Asia, where rice is a staple, rice water (produced by boiling 1 cup of rice in 4 cups of water with a little salt) can be used effectively. In Africa, where wheat and barley are more common, gruel (a thin cereal water) is a great start. Other possible fluids include weak tea, coconut milk, and fruit juices.

These alternatives are generally more palatable than commercially available oral rehydration salts. When a person is ill, food or drink that is unpalatable may also be intolerable. In fact, some people may become even more dehydrated because they do not like the taste of the fluid and the caretaker refuses to consider alternatives.

Use boiled or bottled water if at all possible; but if nothing else is available, don't hesitate to give possibly contaminated fluids. The advantages of rapid fluid replacement far outweigh the disadvantages of contaminated water. As a general rule, adults require two glasses of fluid for each diarrhea stool. For a child, half to one glass is sufficient.

In addition to fluid replacement, Pepto-Bismol, diphenoxylate (Lomotil), or loperamide (Imodium) can be used to treat watery diarrhea. However, these relieve symptoms rather than cure the illness and may in fact prolong the disease. Take them for no longer than two days without receiving medical advice.

For severe diarrhea with blood and mucus, seek medical advice. If you are in a remote area where help is not accessible, take one double strength tablet of trimethoprim-sulphamethoxazole every twelve hours for five days. If diarrhea persists after this period with cramps and abdominal pain and help is still not available, take 750 milligrams of metronidazole (Flagyl) three times a day for seven days.

Many travelers have endured days of diarrhea for lack of basic knowledge regarding how to treat it. People who prepare for nothing else, should be well versed in this problem to prevent long hours of suffering and discomfort.

Coping with Fever

When fever hits and we are far from medical aid, concern for our health often produces panic and a sense of helplessness. Yet not all fevers indicate serious illness. Fevers are caused by a wide range of illnesses from common viral illnesses to malaria and exotic tropical diseases.

If a fever is extremely high (over 102°F), or if it persists for more than a couple of days, seek medical assistance as quickly as possible. In a malarial area where no medical assistance is available and the fever has persisted for more than two days, take three tablets of Fansidar.

As with diarrhea, there are some simple principles for dealing with fever that may relieve discomfort and reduce temperatures regardless of the cause. High fever should be reduced as rapidly as possible, especially in children who may be susceptible to convulsions. Acetaminophen or paracetamol every four hours is important in association with other measures. Aspirin can be used by adults but may cause dangerous side effects in children with fever. Wrapping the patient in a wet sheet and directing a fan across the body is very effective, though the patient may protest when chills set in. Keep the room as cool as possible, or move the patient outside into a cool breezy location if there is no circulation in the room.

It is also important to keep the patient well hydrated with frequent sips of cool drinks. Make sure these contain the necessary electrolytes and calories (see section on diarrhea). Coconut milk or cool fruit juices may be the most appropriate.

Facing a Worldwide Epidemic—HIV/AIDS

Over the past few years I have spent much of my time working in Africa, where the specter of HIV/AIDS is an enormous and frightening reality. Protecting myself and my medical and dental colleagues, many of whom are daily in contact with the blood and bodily secretions of possibly infected patients, is an ever-present problem. HIV/AIDS, or, more properly, Human Immunodeficiency Virus or Auto-immune Deficiency Syndrome, is a lethal disease infecting millions of people throughout the world. The full-blown syndrome may take years to develop but eventually it will kill anyone infected with it.

HIV/AIDS is widespread throughout Africa, the Caribbean (especially Haiti), and increasingly in South America and Asia, where the incidence will soon outstrip that in Africa. It has devastated many communities in developing nations. In some places the number of people infected may be over fifty percent, especially among prostitutes and sexually promiscuous persons. According to some estimates, the two-thirds world will have over eighty percent of the known infections by the year 2000.[1]

Workers in high-risk situations, such as medical and dental clinics, need to take special precautions. Masks, gloves, and protective goggles should be used in all at-risk situations, and counter tops should be cleaned with a one-tenth percent bleach solution after every patient.

Make sure you know the established procedures for handling patients and medical waste to reduce the risk of exposure to this fatal virus. More detailed advice and protocols should be established for your specific situation.

Any missionary organization working in high AIDS areas needs a policy to cover not only the treatment of persons known to have AIDS, but also the possibility of workers contracting the disease from exposure to these patients. MAP International has excellent material regarding the development of policies and the establishment of procedures. They publish a helpful bimonthly bulletin regarding AIDS through their headquarters in Brunswick, Georgia.

AIDS prevention is one of the most frustrating situations I face in overseas service. Many Western workers become as fatalistic and unconcerned as local personnel, often ignoring the simple measures they can take to protect themselves.

One of my friends who works in an obstetrics ward in Kenya refuses to use gloves and goggles for deliveries because they

are not easily available and she does not want to appear different from the locals. However, she has many friends in Europe who would gladly meet her needs as well as those of her colleagues if she would simply let them know her predicament.

One rare situation travelers in developing nations may face is the need for an emergency blood transfusion or any intramuscular or intravenous injection. Those traveling in high-risk areas should carry an "AIDS kit"—a selection of needles, syringes, and I.V. fluids that could be used in such a situation. This is especially true if you are going to a remote area where the sterility of local injections is in doubt. Carry a prescription with you to explain the presence of these items.

Allow a blood transfusion only if you are sure the blood has been screened not only for the HIV virus but also for hepatitis and other viruses. If you're not sure, allow a transfusion only in a life or death situation. Then move the patient as soon as possible to a safe hospital.

Your local embassy is probably the best source of information regarding HIV screening and the availability of "safe" blood. If you are traveling to a remote area, check with the embassy in the capital city before leaving to see what advice they have regarding emergency situations.

If you require hospitalization for such an emergency, or for any other reason, a mission hospital with Western trained doctors or a university affiliated teaching hospital in a major city is most likely to practice Western-style medicine with safe blood supplies.

AIDS Kit Checklist

☐ 5 x 2cc syringes   ☐ 5 x 5cc syringes

☐ 2 x 10cc syringes   ☐ 20 x 21G needles

☐ Exam gloves   ☐ Blood type card

If you are traveling with a medically trained person, add:

☐ I.V. fluids   ☐ I.V. tubing

If you will be part of a large group of people spending a long period of time in a remote area at high risk for AIDS, consider developing your own blood donor pool (which we call a "walking blood bank"). Each traveler should be blood-typed and tested for HIV and HBV (Hepatitis B) antibodies before leaving, and each should carry a card containing blood type and other relevant information.

Smaller groups or individual travelers should contact the local embassy or consulate to acquire information about a volunteer walking blood bank in the country.

Surviving Where There Is No Doctor

One chapter cannot give a comprehensive list of illnesses you might encounter in your travels. All it can do is raise your awareness of potential problems and provide enough information to enable you to ask the right questions and acquire the right resources as you prepare.

At some point, you may need more detailed information when no doctor is available. Americans are so used to having medical advice available twenty-four hours at the other end of a phone line that we panic at the thought of being away from it.

Fortunately, most ailments we suffer from are easy to treat even when no medical practitioner is around, and resource books are available specifically for such occasions. One good resource to help you identify and treat medical complaints is the book *Where There Is No Doctor*.[2] It is written for laypeople, or those with only basic medical knowledge, and contains much valuable information. Another useful pocket-sized book for those with a little more medical knowledge is Elaine Jong's *The Travel and Tropical Medicine Manual*.[3]

CHAPTER 4

Surviving in a Stress-filled Environment

Maintaining Emotional Health

W E ALL live in a stress-filled world, but no one is more aware of it than one who travels to new places and unknown situations.

The constant changes and readjustments to new diets, new cultures, new languages, and new illnesses put them in the high-stress risk zone. Physical danger, isolation, and separation from friends and familiar environments also contribute to high stress. Violent death by accident, homicide, and suicide is also a very real concern in some areas, and the isolation and separation caused by bereavement add to the list of possible emotional problems.

Arriving in a country where I do not speak the language always generates a high level of stress for me. I dread having to face crowded customs halls and aggressive immigration officials, particularly when I am alone and have been traveling for long hours over several time zones.

The border crossing between Ghana and Togo in West Africa holds particularly nightmarish memories for me. No sooner had we stepped out of our taxi than we were surrounded by a swarm of porters shouting and arguing about who would carry our luggage. A tiny African woman, far from young, finally won the battle and, much to my amazement, managed to balance one large suitcase on her head and firmly grasp the other two bags in her hands. She staggered slightly, gained her balance, and soon stood erect, seemingly undisturbed by her huge load. We headed to the immigration facility pushing and shoving our way through the crowd of vendors selling oranges, sweets, and bread.

People jostled for position around the Togolese official who painstakingly wrote each of our names in his little immigration book. Fortunately, our porter knew her job well and quickly pushed her way to the front of the crowd, waving our documents under the eyes of the long-suffering official. He spoke no English, and our attempts to explain the purpose of our visit had little effect.

We were just beginning to relax when the next obstacle confronted us. Due to political unrest in Togo everyone was being searched before entry. So we waited, not too patiently, in the scorching sun and draining humidity for our turn. After two hours of frustration and discomfort we emerged on the Togolese side of the border only to be pounced on by another excited crowd offering us taxis, wanting to change money, or trying to sell local fruit and cigarettes.

Finally we caught sight of our host and, with an enormous sigh of relief, almost collapsed into his arms.

Such events always raise my anxiety levels, though I no longer have to fight an overwhelming desire to turn around and run home.

According to the scale established by Holmes and Masusu to estimate the stress of various life experiences, this and similar episodes put people involved in international missions at high risk for stress. We should be emotional basket cases due to constant changes in financial status, occupation, geographic location, recreational outlets, church routine, social activities, and eating habits.

But the amazing thing is that overall we experience an incredible degree of stability. It doesn't come naturally, though. We need to identify the factors that create it and work to maintain it.

Unfortunately, some missionaries have to leave the field because of burnout and exhaustion. And some, though they stay, carry with them a burden of guilt and frustration because of their inability to meet the needs around them or live up to their own impossible expectations. They become bitter and disillusioned with their work and their organization, and their experiences become negative rather than positive.

Surviving Culture Shock

People arriving in a strange culture feel disoriented because their cultural maps and guidelines no longer work. Stripped of normal ways of coping with life, they are confused, afraid, and angry. They can't even identify what has gone wrong, much less figure out how to deal with it.

The first shock is the inability to communicate. We struggle to say the simplest things and constantly make mistakes. We look foolish and are misunderstood. Our education and intelligence, the symbols that gave us status and security at home, no longer have any meaning. Even when we think we speak the same language and let down our guard, we are in for some unpleasant surprises.

As an Australian living with Americans, I have often been embarrassed, or caused embarrassment, by my use of inappropriate words. On the other hand, I have been offended by words used by Americans that are considered vulgar in Australia. For example, a new and fashionable piece of equipment used in overseas travel is what Americans call "a fanny pouch," a small purse attached to a waistband. When I first heard this expression I almost fainted on the spot. *Fanny* is an extremely offensive word in Australian culture, and it was a long time before I could hear someone use it without subconsciously feeling offended.

Changes in routine can also contribute to culture shock. Frustration mounts when it takes twice as long to do even the simplest task as it did at home.

Changes in relationships are even more difficult to deal with because they are at the center of all human activity and they are necessary for stability. Even family relationships change as each person deals with his or her own stresses and conflicts.

People often become stubborn and rude, withdrawn, or hypocritical in an attempt to reestablish some of their values.

One of my greatest struggles when I started working with Americans was the freedom and abandon with which they seemed to spend money. My American friends often spent money for items I thought they could have made or wasted limited funds on repairs they could have done. On the other hand, my determination to "do it myself" and save a few dollars no matter how long a job took often exasperated them.

It took a long time for me to realize that the conflict involved two different value systems. Americans value time highly and will often spend money to make efficient use of this commodity. Australians on the other hand place a higher value on money and will often criticize Americans for seemingly poor stewardship in this area. Neither value system is right or wrong. They are just different, and it was important for all of us to come to an acceptance of the others' values.

Culture shock is a normal process that all people experience when thrown into new and unfamiliar situations. For some it passes quickly; for others it is a long and unpleasant struggle that may color their view of ministry and overseas service for the rest of their lives.

In *Anthropological Insights for Missionaries*[1], Paul Hiebert likens the adjustment process to that of stages in a marriage.

1. The honeymoon. At this stage everything is new and exciting. This may last for a couple of weeks or for several months. Most short-term missionaries rarely get beyond this stage and their constant exuberance and excitement may be an irritation to long-term workers.

2. Disillusionment. This stage often sets in when we begin to establish our place in the community. Frustration, anger, and anxiety take over our initial starry-eyed exuberance as we begin to cope with language, transportation, and poor sanitation. We compare everything unfavorably to "the way things are at home." We long to go home and often resist only because we don't know how to use the local phone system to call for help. This stage marks the crisis in long-term adjustment. Most people throw away their letters of resignation and begin to relax, but some are unable to cope with the transition and return home bitter and critical.

3. Resolution. This stage is often marked by returning humor and an ability to laugh at ourselves and our predicament. We begin to accept and appreciate our new friends and hosts and start to learn their culture and become one of them. If we remain aloof, we will remain foreigners, and the gospel we proclaim will always be distant and incomprehensible.

4. Adjustment. This stage is marked by our ability to feel comfortable in the new culture without anxiety, fear, or anger. We accept local ways and begin to enjoy them. When we leave, we will miss our new country as much as we missed our own on arrival.

Keys to Emotional Survival

The following six factors have been of immeasurable aid in my quest for mental stability in stressful environments.

1. Maintain spiritual well-being. As already mentioned, a strong Christian commitment has been shown by many organizations to be extremely important in a person's ability to cope in difficult situations. The stronger our faith and ability to trust in Christ Jesus, the greater our tolerance of stress. Daily prayer and Bible study and regular Christian fellowship help us grow spiritually and maintain our foundations. They are as important to our health and well-being as any medicines we may carry.

For me, one of the keys to coping overseas was learning

that it was not wrong to take time out in the middle of the morning to pray for ten minutes or to open my Bible and meditate on the scriptures. At first I felt guilty when I scheduled time to meditate, as though I was wasting "work" time doing something useless. Even though I often worked late into the night, I found it difficult to regard the hours between 8 A.M. and 5 P.M. as being for anything other than work. I eventually realized however that if Christ is the center of my life, He must also be the center of my work. Stopping my physical labors to spend a few moments with Him is as important as the time I spend speaking to my colleagues.

2. Learn to depend on others. None of us is superhuman. We all need others to help us maintain our emotional and physical health. Therefore, it is not wrong to share our problems with others; it is a necessity. Our society is very individualistic and tries to convince us we should be able to cope on our own. However, we are not made to be independent; we're made to be *inter*dependent. God intended that we would need each other. He intended that we would share our problems and draw strength and encouragement from people around us. At the same time we are to provide strength, encouragement, and comfort for our colleagues.

One of the tremendous blessings for me of community life on board the *Anastasis* was the strong friendships I developed. Through these I received support when I was insecure or discouraged, experienced healing for the scars and problems I carried from my past, and developed confidence and patience for the unexpected tasks I had to perform. At times I felt very vulnerable as I confessed my weaknesses and doubts, but such vulnerability gave me the freedom I needed to lean on others and helped me develop spiritually and emotionally in ways I had never even dreamed possible.

3. Accept your own limitations. People who commit themselves to overseas service are often high achievers. They find it difficult to sit still and do nothing. They are constantly on the move and many never learned to say "No." They feel guilty if they take time off or feel the need to slow down. At the same time they try to live up to the perceived expectations of colleagues and fellow churchgoers who are convinced that anyone who goes overseas to work must be physically, emotionally, and spiritually strong.

To maintain our emotional health, we need to recognize symptoms of overwork so we can take the necessary steps to overcome them.

First of all, there is nothing wrong with telling our friends and leaders when we have reached our capacity to cope. All of us have limitations and when we push beyond them, we often pay a high price, first in irritability, then in alienation from friends and colleagues, and eventually in physical or emotional breakdown. We often blame our leaders and co-workers for our own inabilities and are afraid to admit we have limits and weaknesses. As a result, we often transfer our stresses and frustrations to our leaders and accuse them of making us work too hard. Then we jeopardize not only our own health but theirs as well.

An important step for me was realizing that I alone knew my capabilities. Others could give me advice and help me set boundaries, but unless I was willing to admit I was not coping under stress there was no way those around me could know what my needs were. I constantly fell into the trap of committing myself to more than I could possibly do in the time available. Then I would feel inadequate and discouraged when I failed to finish my commitments. Next would come grumbling and criticism from those around me who had not noticed how overloaded I was.

It was a wonderful release for me to share this problem and have others help me realistically look at what I could achieve in a given time period. It not only made my work load lighter, but also gave me permission to enjoy my time off.

Another thing that helped me tremendously was realizing that even Jesus knew when to stop and turn away from the endless stream of people demanding His attention. At times He retreated into the hills to pray and sometimes He walked to another village, leaving needs unmet in the place He had vacated. He always was confident of the job God had called Him to do and used that as the basis for His daily decisions.

Another great help was a psychological test called "Myers Briggs." It helped me understand my strengths and weaknesses, pointed out areas where I needed help, and suggested the type of people who would best be able to help me. A psychological test such as this is a real asset to anyone planning to spend a long period of time working overseas.

4. Learn to expect and cope with change. Few things in life remain stable when we travel. We constantly change our location, financial basis, and friendships. Yet it is the stable points that contribute most to emotional equilibrium. It is important, therefore, to identify and protect these.

My understanding of this was greatly enhanced by reading Lyle Schaller's *Strategies For Change*.[2] I have adapted here some of the principles I learned from his excellent book.

a. Identify the stable points in your life. It may be something as simple as a regular schedule for meals and Bible study or a friendship that has seen you through thick and thin. Whatever it is, hang on to it.

b. Maintain as much stability as possible. You may be tempted to move to a new place that is larger, prettier, or quieter, but before doing so think about the stresses this change will add to your life and weigh those against the pressures it may ease.

One of the most destabilizing events in my life was when I began to do a lot of air travel away from the *Anastasis*. At the same time there was an accident in my cabin that made it unlivable for several months. Every time I returned to the ship I stayed in a different cabin. I soon found that having a constantly moving object as my only point of reference made me disoriented and unable to cope with all that was going on around me.

c. Surround yourself with items that give an "at home" feeling. The more you can do to feel comfortable in the new environment, the less stressful it will seem and the easier your emotional adjustment will be. For me, a painting of Sydney harbor hanging in my cabin was a great focus for "at home" feelings.

d. Establish friendships that have the potential to be stable. If you plan to spend a long period of time in a place, it is no good to establish friendships only with people who are there for a short time. Constantly developing new friendships is exhausting and emotionally draining. Consciously build relationships that help maintain a stable environment.

e. Identify "enemy factors" and ways to deal with them.

Learn which people, foods, or climates make you uncomfortable and figure out ways to avoid or cope with them.

f. Affirm the good; don't concentrate on the bad. Bad news tends to travel faster than good news, so work at concentrating on the positive as much as possible so that your thoughts are not heavily weighted in the negative.

g. Avoid surprises. The normal response to sudden change is rejection, so the ability to predict coming changes makes it easier to adjust to them. When you arrive, ask other people what factors or events took them by surprise and prepare yourself for them. Listen to what is happening around you so that you are not hit by sudden change—even a day's preparation can make a tremendous difference in the ability to cope.

5. Cultivate meaningful leisure time. Most high achievers enjoy work and take little time for pleasure. We all need to know what activities refresh us emotionally, physically, and spiritually and to make sure we spend adequate leisure time engaged in these activities. As an extrovert, I enjoy people-related activities as a means of revitalizing, so I try to plan a party, a visit to the market, or a trip to the beach with friends on my days off. An introvert, however, will prefer reading, writing, or quietly listening to music.

Most of us want to get out and see as much of a new country as possible, particularly if we are there for only a short period of time. It is fun to visit new places, meet new people, and develop new friendships. Yet these activities are exhausting and deplete our physical and emotional reserves as we struggle to communicate in an unfamiliar language or jostle through disruptive crowds. We often neglect sleep and spiritual discipline to pursue them and in the long run they may make us depressed, angry, and irritable.

Sleep is also important. Getting enough of it can make an incredible difference in the ability to cope with pressure. The heat, humidity, and noise in many tropical areas often make this difficult. If you are run down due to lack of sleep, do not be afraid to check into an air-conditioned hotel for a weekend to catch up on the hours you missed during the week. It may make all the difference in your ability to cope.

When Jesus' disciples returned after their first preaching and healing mission, Jesus listened to their reports and then said, "Come aside by yourself to a deserted place and rest a while." This is important advice for all of us to follow after a highly emotional and stressful ministry time.

I also love the story of Elijah in the wilderness (1 Kings 19:1–9). Here we have the perfect picture of a stressed out person after intense ministry. He wanted to die. He was physically and mentally exhausted after his gruelling escape from Jezebel. He was alone, his body ached, and he had no will to continue. And what did God do? He gave him food and sleep before correcting him and sending him back on his journey.

6. Take time out regularly to evaluate spiritual and practical goals and priorities. I have found it to be essential for my physical, emotional, and spiritual health to take a day every three to four months and retire to a place far away from my duties to re-evaluate my priorities. Adequate evaluation cannot be done in the midst of a busy work schedule. It is important to move physically away from our place of work to do such an evaluation. You may check into a hotel for a couple of days, for instance, to do your evaluation.

We need not wait until we are overseas to begin this type of retreat. In fact, they are a wonderful addition to life here and now. My husband and I try to take a couple of days for a spiritual retreat every three or four months to make sure our lives are "on line" physically and spiritually as far as our commitments are concerned.

During your pre-trip retreat, list your job priorities and other important aspects of your life, including prayer and Bible study, leisure time, family time, and time for household chores. This will give you a foundation on which to base your activities and time while away. Otherwise the busyness and pressures of your overseas trip will make it impossible to see clearly.

When I started traveling extensively overseas, I did not stop to consider the implications of the heavy schedule I set myself. I flew to a new destination on Sunday, had meetings Monday through Friday, and then flew to my next destination during the weekend. I soon found that both my physical and mental health were suffering from such a crazy way of life, yet it was very difficult to break out of the routine I had established for myself.

When I finally took time out to sit down with a friend and look at my commitments I realized how ridiculous my way of life was. I added to my schedule time for recreation, reserved a day after arrival for adaptation to a new environment and the effects of jetlag, allowed time after a trip to catch up on household chores, and generally gave myself the freedom to relax and enjoy life again. I soon found my efficiency increased rather than decreased because I was more alert and rested when I appeared for work. I also learned the importance of seeking counsel and the value of sharing my weaknesses and sense of failure with others.

It is good to repeat this process every three to four months during a trip overseas since priorities change and we lose our focus. I ask myself the following questions, though I admit it is not always easy to give myself honest answers.

1. Am I satisfied with my spiritual state and development? What am I doing regularly to maintain or improve that state? All of us like to feel that we measure up to God's expectations, but we rarely take time to assess our progress. Prayer and Bible study fade away or become perfunctory in the presence of more immediate demands on our time, yet without them we soon become dry and brittle, unable to bend under the pressures of life. I need to take adequate time on a regular basis not just to read the Bible but also to study it in depth. When I am too tired or too busy, I know I have allowed my priorities to become misplaced.

2. What am I doing regularly to maintain my physical well-being? Regular exercise improves physical strength and emotional well-being, and it should be an integral part of our routine. This is not always easy in the two-thirds world where health clubs and jogging paths do not exist. However, there are always opportunities to walk, and exercise programs can be adapted to any situation you are in.

3. How adequately am I covering my work responsibilities? What can I do to improve my performance and maintain an efficient working environment? Eighty percent of work is completed in twenty percent of the time we spend on it. The other eighty percent is less focused and less effective. Therefore, we could eliminate much from our schedules if we had a clear view of our purpose and calling. When I feel pressured in my work, I learn to ask God what He really expects of me. I have also learned the importance of asking for input from friends who know and understand my limitations.

4. What are my relationships with my colleagues, family, and friends like? Ruptured relationships often indicate that I am "over the limit" stress-wise and tell me I need to make changes in my routine. When we begin blaming others for our mistakes or become irritable and critical, particularly of our leaders, it is a pretty clear indication that we've lost our focus.

5. What am I doing with my time off? Do I make sure I get adequate leisure time to maintain my equilibrium? The protestant work ethic tends to give low priority to rest and relaxation. We are constantly on the go—watching the clock, counting statistics as a measure of our effectiveness, and generally pressuring ourselves to do more and work longer hours. We have a lot to learn from our friends in the two-thirds world who are relationship oriented rather than task oriented. These people are much better at taking time for rest and relaxation than we are.

This has been an extremely difficult area for me to come to terms with. I have always felt guilty for scheduling leisure time as part of my routine because it seems like a waste of time. However, I have learned over the past few years that it is essential for my physical, emotional, and spiritual well-being, and I now enjoy relaxation without feeling guilt or condemnation.

6. *What records do I keep to help me plan and evaluate my life and achievements?* A diary, written in regularly, is of great benefit in assessing spiritual, emotional, and practical progress. You may want to divide it into sections for spiritual, practical, and relationship goals and then write insights, struggles, and a progress report each week. When you go on your retreats, these will give you a good basis for evaluation and reflection.

7. *Do I have someone with whom I can share my joys and frustrations? To whom can I go for advice and counsel? With whom can I be vulnerable and weak? Who really knows me as I am?* We desperately need others to help in our adaptation to overseas environments, yet we are so used to being independent that we are afraid to reach out and commit ourselves to this type of relationship. I cannot emphasize enough how important it is.

Our response under stress may be one of the greatest testimonies of our Christian faith, not because we react perfectly in the midst of it but because in its presence we face our fallibility and weakness and learn to rely on God and allow Him to change us in ways we never would while we are comfortable.

The above principles come mainly from my own experience. I have pushed myself beyond my limits and learned to draw back. I have increased my own burdens and blamed others. I have become ill, depressed, and burned out and almost given up my involvement in overseas service. Through it all I have learned, and continue to learn, that I am often my own worst enemy when coping under stress and in difficult situations. I am seeing more and more that I will grow and change only as I look to God for the solutions.

Under pressure we have two choices. We can either draw closer to God through the difficulties we face or we can draw back and become bitter and disillusioned. Pressure and stress can increase our faith and trust. It can strengthen our areas of weakness and increase our interdependence with others or it can send us away from God, away from a growing knowledge of ourselves, and away from service for Him. Each of us holds the key to our future and to the lessons we will learn from our struggles.

CHAPTER 5

Surviving Reentry

Health Hints for the Returning Traveler

MANY VOLUNTEERS return home with unidentified illnesses lurking in their bodies. International travel places stress on bodies, emotions, and spirits, and often the full implications are not apparent until we return home.

A bout of diarrhea, which may have eluded you throughout your trip, may strike after you return home. If it persists, or if you had recurrent bouts during your travels, consult your local doctor and be tested for giardiasis, amoebiasis, and typhoid, which are possible causes of prolonged diarrhea.

Individuals who lived in remote areas in developing nations for six months or more may want to repeat the skin test for tuberculosis. And travelers who have been away several months may want to take a routine dose of mebendazole (Vermox). One tablet daily for three days will cure round worms and other helminth infections that are rampant in many developing nations. A similar course of treatment every six to twelve months for those who spend prolonged periods of time in such countries is also wise. This medication is usually available as an over-the-counter drug. For children, piperazine liquid may be preferred.

Those who have spent time in malarial areas need to be aware that this infection may take several months to manifest itself and can occur even if the stay has been as brief as a few hours. In fact, cases of malaria have been reported in people living near major airports in Europe, where the offending mosquitoes have "deplaned" after "hitchhiking" from Africa.

If a high fever occurs within twelve months of returning from a malarial area, seek immediate medical attention.

The first case of malaria I treated was a young man who had visited Belize eight months earlier. Ron had taken his medication religiously throughout his stay and during the post-trip period. Fortunately, when his fevers of 105°F and higher began, we thought of malaria immediately because we knew his history of traveling in Belize. Had we not known where he had been this diagnosis would never have occurred to us.

Any fever, bout of diarrhea, or serious illness that occurs in the first twelve months after returning from a developing nation may be the result of insidious infections acquired during your stay. This possibility should always be mentioned to your local doctor. A physician cannot treat you appropriately if you keep him or her in the dark about your activities.

Emotional and spiritual problems may also surface after your return. These are often just as real but less tangible and more difficult to admit to.

For several years in a row I returned to the United States a few days before Christmas. The contrast between the dirt and squalor of the two-thirds world and the opulence and materialism of the West was almost more than I could bear. Although I was returning home to celebrate the coming of a Savior who gave up the wealth and beauty of heaven to suffer and die for us, I felt no joy. Instead I felt angry when I saw people's indifference to the starving millions of our world and I felt guilty about my own abundance. On top of that, people rarely wanted to listen to what I had learned and could not identify with the changes that had occurred in my heart.

Coming to terms with such contrasts and resisting the pressures of our culture to conform to a way of life that has very different values from the kingdom of God is never easy. It raises many important questions in our minds that may require good counselors to help us work through.

Those of us who work overseas often return with deep emotional needs that require professional counseling. The stressful way of life, the constant change, and the overwhelming pressures all take their toll. And the adjustments back into our own culture and society can be as real and as difficult as the initial adjustments on the field. Amazingly, this can be as true after a short trip as after many years. We are changed by our experiences, and there is no way back. Upon returning, we learn that our experiences have separated us from friends and colleagues. The pressures build until we are unable to cope with our reactions on our own. Missionaries are not superhumans, though churches often treat them as such.

Re-entry[1] by Peter Jordan is an excellent book to read when you return. It will help you find your way through the readjustment period.

Another helpful therapy is getting together with others who have had similar experiences. Seek out returned missionaries or people who have spent years overseas working in secular jobs. Find out from the organization you worked with if other returned missionaries live in your area. A visit with them could help you regain your emotional equilibrium.

You may even want to explore with your co-workers the possibility of returning together to one area rather than returning to separate homes. The shared experiences and strong emotional and spiritual bonds that develop in overseas service are often lifelong, and the transition back into "normal" life may be much easier if you do it as a group rather than alone.

There is much we can do to educate our churches and our friends about the new world that opened before us and changed our lives. When we first return, people are enthusiastic about seeing our slides and hearing of our experiences. But their enthusiasm wanes long before our desire to share does. We can easily become depressed and listless in response to this seeming rejection.

Instead of allowing this to happen, look for some creative approaches that will allow you to continue bringing the needs of the less fortunate before your friends. Prepare a meal like those you ate overseas and dress in native costume; ask the pastor if you can start a missionary prayer group; organize a hunger awareness walk; or find out how you can plug into existing church groups and organizations in your area that are involved in missions. World Relief has produced an excellent series of studies entitled "Feed the Poor" that is geared for different age groups.[2] I highly recommend these as a means of raising missions awareness in your church.

Other important groups to connect with are the prayer partners and support teams that made your trip possible. Your experience overseas should be as much of an encouragement to them as it was for you.

As soon as you return, start making changes in your own life that prove that your experiences have altered your values and given you new priorities. If your friends see that your experiences have made a real and permanent positive change in your life they are much more likely to take notice.

Study what Scripture has to say about the poor and our

responsibility for them. Such knowledge carries with it some radical implications regarding lifestyle and priorities and without a biblical basis, many of us will slip back into a familiar way of life and soon forget the resolves we made to be less materialistic and self-centered.

Books that helped me in this area were Ron Sider's *Rich Christians in an Age of Hunger*[3] and Donald Kraybill's *The Upside Down Kingdom.*[4] Another excellent resource is *Live It Up! How to Create a Life You Can Love*[5] by Tom Sine.

One of the common operations we perform on board the Anastasis is the repair of a cleft lip. Patients line up at the beginning of the ship's visit, hopeful of receiving help for this ugly deformity that has left them ostracized and rejected by their family and peers.

After the operation many of them sit looking in a mirror for hours, trying to convince themselves that the normal face they see is really their own. I love to watch the wide grin that spreads across their faces and the new light that sparkles in their eyes as they realize the transformed face in the mirror does indeed belong to them. That look is ample reward for all my hard work and inconvenience.

Personally, I cannot imagine a life more fulfilling than one committed to overseas service. The joy and satisfaction I have experienced as a result of meeting the medical needs of people who had no other hope of healing is far more important than the financial reward I would have received if I had continued my medical practice in Christchurch, New Zealand.

Maintaining Spiritual Balance

FINALLY BE strong in the Lord and in his mighty power. Put on the full armor of God so that you can take your stand against the devil's schemes. For our struggle is not against flesh and blood, but against the rulers, against the authorities, against the powers of this dark world and against the spiritual forces of evil in the heavenly realms" (Ephesians 6:10–12).

Whenever we travel overseas, the possibility of ill health is something we need to face and be willing to accept. Modern medicine and immunizations can guard against many diseases that once killed millions of people, yet others remain unconquered. Like missionaries of old, we must understand that no price is too high to pay to spread the wonderful news of the gospel of Jesus Christ.

I have always admired missionaries who willingly sacrificed everything, including their health and sometimes their lives, to spread the gospel to unknown lands. They had no airplanes to provide a fast escape if an epidemic hit. They had no modern drugs to fight infections such as typhoid, cholera, and malaria, and no vaccines to provide protection from polio, measles, and tetanus.

For many of them, a call to the mission field meant they would never again see their homes or families. For others it meant they would complete life riddled with devastating diseases that robbed them of their vitality and health.

The Moravian missionaries were a particularly dedicated group who took up the challenge in Africa even though many lived only a short time after their arrival. So committed were they to the cause of spreading the gospel that they were willing to make any sacrifice to preach the Good News. Some even packed their clothes in coffins instead of suitcases, accepting before their departure the inevitability of death.

Father Damien, who worked among the lepers on the island of Molokai, Hawaii, is another whose dedication ignored the risk. After many years, he too contracted and succumbed to the terrifying disease. Only in the midst of his suffering did the lepers really start to listen to his message about a God who loved them so much that He sent someone to share their disease.

It is such dedication that God expects from all Christians. In spite of our precautions and preparations, we must still be willing to take risks. Neither good health nor life itself is more important than obedience to the call God places on our lives. Having considered the risks, we must be willing to continue on the pathway He sets before us, joyfully embracing the pain and suffering that may result.

We are called to touch people's lives, to reach out with love and compassion to those around us who are bound by sin, sickness, and poverty. Sometimes that is impossible to do without tasting of life as they live it. Obedience to the will of God is far more important than physical health. Fear of illness and death should never control the way we act or minister.

Having done all we can to protect ourselves, we must continue to move along the pathway He has marked out for us, accepting His grace to guide us through whatever the future holds. Sometimes He will graciously extend His hand of protection over us, keeping us from all illness. At other times we go down like flies before the onslaught of local germs, groping desperately for an understanding of our woes.

Whatever happens, we must learn in this, as in all else, to accept that He orders our steps for His purposes. His ways are far higher than ours. Our confidence is in Him, not in our health or in the precautions we have taken.

Nothing God asks us to do should ever be too hard for us to accept. No place He asks us to go, no sacrifice He asks us to make will ever be too great to consider for the sake of our Savior Jesus Christ. He gave up the wonder of life in heaven to enter the pain and misery of our world so that through Him we might know salvation and the wonder of renewed relationship with God. May our commitment to others be as great as His is to us.

Checklists

Pre-trip Checklist

☐ Medical visit   ☐ Immunizations

☐ Malarial prophylaxis   ☐ First-aid kit

☐ Dental check   ☐ Check packing

First-aid Kit Checklist

☐ Band-aids   ☐ Insect repellent

☐ Hydrogen peroxide   ☐ Sunscreen

☐ Sterile gauze   ☐ Antihistamines

☐ Cotton swabs   ☐ Pain-killers

☐ Water filter   ☐ Water purifier tablets

☐ Antibiotics   ☐ Antifungal tablets

☐ Antifungal cream or   ☐ Antimalarials
  powder

☐ Metronidazole   ☐ Antidiarrheals

☐ Laxatives   ☐ Anti-motion sickness
                             medication

☐ Sleeping pills   ☐ Ear plugs

☐ Talcum powder   ☐ Prescription medications

Packing Checklist

☐ Cotton clothing ☐ Long pants or skirt

☐ Long-sleeved shirt ☐ Dress clothes

☐ Toiletries ☐ Cotton underwear

☐ Sweater ☐ Raincoat

☐ Walking shoes ☐ First-aid kit

☐ Broad-brimmed hat ☐ Sunglasses

☐ Water canteen ☐ Mosquito net

☐ Water filter ☐ Camera

☐ Bible ☐ Reference books

☐ 110/220 V converter ☐ Appropriate electrical adaptor

☐ "At-home" items ☐ Prescription medications

☐ AIDS kit (see page70) ☐ Towels

☐ Bedding ☐ Special hand luggage items (see separate list)

Hand Luggage Checklist

- [ ] Airplane & other tickets
- [ ] Passport
- [ ] Facial tissues
- [ ] Flashlight
- [ ] Razor and razorblades
- [ ] Prescription medications
- [ ] Nail file
- [ ] Water canteen
- [ ] Sunglasses
- [ ] Scissors

- [ ] Yellow immunization card
- [ ] Local address
- [ ] Wet wipes
- [ ] Sewing kit
- [ ] Comb
- [ ] Toothbrush & toothpaste
- [ ] Swiss Army knife
- [ ] Eyeglasses
- [ ] Hat
- [ ] Pain-killers

Spiritual Checklist (Psalm 51:10–12)

"A clean heart"	Forgiveness and reconciliation
"A steadfast spirit"	Endurance and perseverance
"Your presence"	Fellowship with God
"Your Holy Spirit"	Power and comfort
"The joy of your salvation"	Joy and love
"A willing spirit"	Flexibility and obedience

AIDS Kit Checklist

☐ 5 x 2cc syringes   ☐ 5 x 5cc syringes

☐ 2 x 10cc syringes   ☐ 20 x 21G needles

☐ Exam gloves   ☐ Blood type card

If you are traveling with a medically trained person, add:

☐ I.V. fluids   ☐ I.V. tubing

Notes

Introduction

1. Mercy Ships, P.O. Box 2020, Lindale, TX 75771, 1-800-626-7667.

Chapter 1

1. Pan American Health Organization 1992, 525 23rd St., N.W., Washington, D.C. 20037, 202-293-8130.

2. "Health Information for International Travel 1992," U.S. Department of Health & Human Services 1992.

3. "International Travel and Health for 1993," World Health Organization Distribution and Sales, 1211 Geneva 27 Switzerland, or WHO Publication Center, 49 Sheridan Ave., Albany, NY 12210, 518-436-9686.

4. WHO report "Healthlink," June 1993, National Council for International Health, 1701 K St., N.W., Suite 600, Washington, D.C. 20006, 202-833-5900.

5. Center for Disease Control, Atlanta, GA 30333, 404-329-3311.

Chapter 2

1. Recreational Equipment, Inc. (REI), 15400 20th, N.E., Bellevue, WA 98007, 206-643-3700.

2. MAP International, P.O. Box 50, Brunswick, GA 31521-0500, 912-265-6010.

3. Katadyn U.S.A., Inc., 3020 N. Scottsdale Road, Scottsdale, AZ 85251, 602-990-3131 or 800-950-0808.

4. *World Vision Magazine,* World Vision, 919 W. Huntington Dr., Monrovia, CA. 91016.

5. *World Christian,* World Christian, Inc., P.O. Box 3278, Ventura, CA 93006.

6. *Christian Medical & Dental Society Journal,* Vol. XXIII, No. 2, Summer 1992.

Chapter 3

1. WHO statistics 1993, World Health Organization, 1211 Geneva 27, Switzerland, 791-24-76.

2. David Werner, *Where There Is No Doctor,* Hesperian Press.

3. Elaine C. Jong, M.D., *The Travel and Tropical Medicine Manual,* (Philadelphia: W.B. Saunders Company, 1987).

Chapter 4

1. Paul Hiebert, *Anthropological Insights for Missionaries,* (Grand Rapids, MI: Baker, 1985).

2. Lyle Schaller, *Strategies for Change,* (Nashville: Abingdon).

Chapter 5

1. Peter Jordan, *Reentry,* (Seattle: YWAM, 1992).

2. "Feed My People," The Christian's Responsibility to the World's Poor, World Relief, Box WRC, Wheaton, IL 60189, 708-665-0235.

3. Ron Sider, *Rich Christians in an Age of Hunger,* (Downer's Grove: InterVarsity, 1978).

4. Donald Kraybill, *The Upside Down Kingdom,* (Scottsdale, PA: Herald Press, 1978, rev. 1990).

5. Tom Sine, *Live It Up! How to Create a Life You Can Love,* (Scottsdale, PA: Herald Press, 1993).